Doctors Jokes

The Ultimate Collection of !

By Chester Croker

Jokes For Doctors

Here we present a huge collection of the very best doctors jokes and puns which will prove that laughter really is the best medicine. These jokes for doctors will hit your funny bone and put you in stitches.

These are the very best doctors jokes and puns which will prove that doctors have a great sense of humor, and these jokes are guaranteed to make you laugh out loud.

There are some great one-liners to start with, plenty of quick fire question and answer themed gags, many story led jokes and plenty of doctor-patient exchanges all designed to get you laughing.

There was going to be a joke about surgeons, but they asked me to take it out.

Published by Glowworm Press
7 Nuffield Way
Abingdon OX14 1RL

Disclaimer
All rights reserved. No part of this publication may be reproduced in any form or by any means without the written permission of the publisher. The information herein is offered for informational purposes only, and is universal as so. The presentation of the information is without contract or any type of guarantee assurance. Under no circumstances will any legal responsibility or blame be held against the author for any reparation, damages or monetary loss due to the information herein, either directly or indirectly.

FOREWORD

When I was asked to write a foreword to this book I was flattered.

That is until I was told by the author, Chester Croker, that I was the last resort, and that everyone else he had approached had said they couldn't do it!

I have known Chester for a number of years and his ability to create funny jokes is remarkable. He is incredibly quick witted and an expert at crafting clever puns and amusing gags and I feel he is the ideal man to put together a joke book to inject some fun into your life.

He once told me, "When you're a doctor you must understand that patients are a virtue."

Mind you, my doctor told me I was going deaf. That was four years ago, and I haven't heard from him since.

Enjoy!

Ian Payne

Table of Contents

Chapter 1: One-Liner Doctor Jokes

Chapter 2: Questions and Answers Doctor Jokes

Chapter 3: Shorter Doctor Jokes

Chapter 4: Doctor Patient Exchanges

Chapter 5: Longer Doctor Jokes

Chapter 6: Rude Doctor Jokes

Chapter 7: Not In Theatre

Chapter 8: Doctors Pick-Up Lines

Chapter 9: Bumper Stickers for Doctors

Chapter 10: Summary

Chapter 1: One Liner Doctor Jokes

A couple of years ago my doctor told me I had problems letting go of the past.

My doctor told me that jogging could add years to my life. He was right – I feel five years older already.

My doctor told me not to worry about bird flu. He said it's tweetable.

Yesterday my doctor left me in the waiting room for an hour. I thought, 'He can't treat me like this.'

The doctor who can smile when things go wrong…… is probably going off duty.

Statistically 9 out of 10 injections are in vein.

My psychiatrist said I was pre-occupied with vengeance.

I told him, "Oh yeah, we'll see about that."

When someone asks me if I'm seeing anyone, I automatically assume they're talking about my seeing a psychiatrist.

I'm not a doctor but I know adding cheese to anything makes it an anti-depressant.

My friend had to be rushed into hospital after a freak accident left a gyroscope lodged in his head. Doctors describe his condition as very stable.

I told my doctor, "I have an inferiority complex but it's not a very good one."

Most doctors refer to motorcyclists as 'organ donors.'

A doctor told his patient to stop using a cotton bud, but it went in one ear and out the other.

Yesterday, a doctor's wife asked him to pass her lipstick but he passed her a super-glue stick instead by mistake. She still isn't talking to him.

When an employment application asks who is to be notified in case of emergency, I always write, "A very good doctor."

My doctor told me I should work out, so I've bought myself a calculator.

Did you hear about the guy who stole a calendar from a doctor's office? He got twelve months.

I remember the fear of realizing on the first day of medical school that watching every episode of ER would get me nowhere.

Being a doctor means you can expose yourself to rare and exotic diseases on a regular basis.

Did you hear about the baby born in the high-tech delivery room? It was cordless.

Always thank your doctor. Sometimes they're the only ones between you and a hearse.

I went to the doctor about having a compulsion to make nasty remarks about people and he prescribed me a course of anti-defamatories.

If you know anyone who wants some leaflets on hemorrhoids, point them in my direction - I've got piles.

My doctor gave me some anti-gloating cream. I can't wait to rub it in.

My doctor has told me I'm morbidly obese. Well he's wrong. I may be fat but I'm not upset about it.

Medicine would be a dream job if there were no patients.

You know you are a doctor when you find yourself betting on a patient's blood alcohol content.

When I am shopping, I avoid unhealthy looking people for fear that I may have to administer CPR on my day off.

Medicine is not a career - it's a post-apocalyptic survival skill.

Did you hear about the cross eyed junior doctor who got sacked because he couldn't see eye to eye with his patients.

Last week, my husband wanted to spice things up a little, and he suggested that we play doctors and nurses. So I strapped him to a trolley, put him in the hallway, and ignored him for 6 hours.

Transplant surgeons hate rejection.

A doctor friend of mine gave me some great advice, saying I should put something away for a rainy day. I've gone for an umbrella.

Did you hear about the doctor who died and went to hell? It took him three weeks to realize that he wasn't at work anymore.

You take a blue pill every day, Sir? Well, that narrows it down.

A senior doctor instructs a group of junior doctors, "Be patient with patients who are not patient."

The doctor taking my blood got annoyed when I told him that he was bad at his job. I don't understand why though, as all he kept saying was, "Be negative."

A doctor told a female patient she could no longer touch anything alcoholic.

So she got a divorce.

I went to the doctors and I said, "I've got a rash." He said, "I'll be as quick as I can."

I went to the doctor with a fractured humerus. He said it wasn't funny.

I was accidentally hit on the head by a drummer. The doctor says I'm suffering from percussion.

The doctor said to this kleptomaniac, "Take these tablets 3 times a day, an if there is no change in a week, get me a big TV and an iPhone."

My doctor told me to cut down on starch. He obviously doesn't know how much I hate ironing.

When I told the doctor about my loss of memory, he made me pay in advance.

I went to see my doctor about my insomnia, but the surgery wasn't open at half past three in the morning.

A psychiatrist instructed his nurse, "Please tell people we are busy rather than telling them this is a madhouse."

Yesterday I accidentally swallowed some food colouring. The doctor says I'm OK, but I feel like I've dyed a little inside.

I was called pretty today. Actually, the full sentence was, 'You're a pretty bad doctor' but I'm focusing on the positive.

When I went to get my vaccinations the young doctor told me he was nervous as it was his first time giving injections. I told him to give it his best shot.

Laughter is not the best medicine - Propofol is.

Chapter 2: Question and Answer Doctor Jokes

Q: When does a doctor lose his temper?
A: *When he runs out of patients.*

Q: Why did the pillow go to the doctor?
A: *He was feeling all stuffed up.*

Q: What did one tonsil say to the other tonsil?
A: *I hear the doctor is taking us out tonight.*

Q: What did one tonsil say to the other tonsil?
A: *Get dressed up, the doctor is taking us out.*

Q: Why is a doctor always calm?

A: *Because he has a lot of patients.*

Q: What did the doctor say to the alcoholic?
A: *Keep taking the Pils.*

Q: What's the difference between a general practitioner and a specialist?
A: *One treats what you have, the other thinks you have what he treats.*

Q: What's the difference between a marriage and a mental hospital?
A: *At a mental hospital you have to show some improvement to get out.*

Q: What do you call a doctor that fixes websites?
A: *A URL-ologist.*

Q: What do you call a doctor who is happy every Monday?

A: *Retired.*

Q: What do you call two orthopedic doctors reading an EKG?

A: *A double blind study.*

Q: What do you call a student that got C's all the way through med school?

A: *Hopefully not your doctor.*

Q: What did the patient say to the x-ray technician after swallowing some money?

A: *"Do you see any change in me?"*

Q: Where do sick boats go to get healthy?

A: *To the docks.*

Q: Why did the doctor tell the nurse to walk past the pill cupboard quietly?

A: *So she wouldn't wake the sleeping pills.*

Q: How do you tell the difference between an oral thermometer and a rectal thermometer?

A: *By the taste.*

Q: What happened when the doctor searched for information about impotence on the Internet?

A: *Nothing came up.*

Q: Why did the cannibal doctor get disciplined by his boss?

A: *For buttering up his patients.*

Chapter 3: Short Doctor Jokes

The surgery receptionist informs an anxious patient, "Doctor Wychniewski is ready to see you."

The patient says, "Which doctor?'

The receptionist replies, "Oh, no, he's fully qualified."

A worried nurse said, "Doctor, the man you just gave a clean bill of health to dropped dead just as he was leaving the hospital."

The doctor replied, "Turn him around. Make it look like he was walking in."

I went to casualty yesterday and told the doctor, "I've been stung by a bee, have you got anything for it?"

He asked, "Whereabouts is it?"

I replied, "I don't know, it could be miles away by now."

The doctor was puzzled with a new patient who had just been admitted.

He said, "I am very sorry Mr O'Reilly, but I am unable to diagnose your problem. I think it must be drink."

The patient replied, "Don't worry about it doc. Come back later when you're sober."

A doctor says to an elderly man who is hard of hearing, "We need a stool sample and a urine sample."

The husband asks his wife, "What did she say?"

His wife replies, "They want your underwear."

A senior civil servant went to the doctor and complained of being unable to sleep.

The doctor asked, "Do you sleep at night?"

The civil servant replied, "Yes, I sleep very well at night. I sleep quite soundly most of the mornings, too - but I find it is very difficult to sleep in the afternoons as well."

The doctor says, "I have got some bad news for you. You've got six months to live."

The horrified patient says, "Six months? Doc, I can't pay your bill in six months, I simply can't do it."

The doctor replies, "OK, I give you a year."

A guy goes to the doctor with a hearing problem.

The doctor says, "Can you describe the symptoms to me?"

The guy replies, "Yes. Homer is a fat yellow lazy man and his wife Marge is skinny with big blue hair."

A man walks into a doctor's office.

He has a cucumber up his nose, a banana in his left ear and a carrot in his right ear.

He asks the doctor, "What's the matter with me?"

The doctor replies, "You're not eating properly."

A nervous hospital patient says, "Doctor, are you sure I'm suffering from malaria? I once heard about a doctor treating someone with malaria and he died of typhus."

The doctor replies, "Don't worry, it won't happen to you. If I treat someone with malaria, he will die of malaria."

A 75 years old retired doctor was walking in the park one day when he came across a frog.

He reached down, picked the frog up, and went to put it into his jacket.

As he did so, the frog said, "Kiss me on the lips and I'll turn into a beautiful woman and show you a really good time."

The old doctor carried on putting the frog in his pocket.

The frog croaked, "Didn't you hear what I said?"

The retired doctor looked at the frog and said, "Yes, but at my age I would prefer to have a talking frog."

A young woman wearing Gothic clothing, numerous tattoos and with a purple Mohican punk rocker hairstyle bursts into the hospital complaining of abdominal pain.

The doctor quickly established that the patient had acute appendicitis, so she was booked in for immediate surgery.

When she was completely disrobed on the operating table, the staff observed that her pubic hair had been dyed green, and above it, there was a tattoo that read, 'Keep off the grass.'

After the surgery had been completed, the surgeon wrote a short note on the patient's dressing, which said, 'Sorry, but I had to mow the lawn.'

A man goes to a doctor complaining of several issues.

The doctor does his diagnosis and eventually says, "I've got very bad news - you've got cancer and dementia."

The patient says, "Well, at least I don't have cancer."

Two men are in a rainforest and one of them is having a wee in the tress.

As he is doing so, a snake slithers and bites the man's penis.

The guy naturally screams out loud.

The other guy sees the snake dangling from the pan's penis and decides to rush back to the field hospital where he know there is a doctor.

The doctor listens to what happened and says, "We do not carry any anti-venom. You will have to go back to your friend, and make an incision at the wound and suck the poison out."

On returning to the guy with the snake bite, he says, "Sorry, but the doctor says there is no cure, and no treatment."

A doctor asked a novice nurse, "Did you take the patient's temperature?"

The novice nurse replies, "No, is it missing?"

A man goes to his doctors.

The doctor says, "I've not seen you for a while."

The man replies, "Yes, I've been ill."

A man goes to the eye doctor.

The man complains, "I keep seeing spots in front of my eyes."

The doctor asks, "Have you ever seen a doctor?"

The man replies, "No, just spots."

The evolution of medicine:

"Doctor, I have an ear ache."

2000 B.C. - Eat this root.
1000 B.C. - That root is heathen, say this prayer.
1850 A.D. - That prayer is superstition, drink this potion.
1940 A.D. - That potion is snake oil, swallow this pill.
1985 A.D. - That pill is ineffective, take this antibiotic.
2000 A.D. - That antibiotic is artificial. Eat this root!

A man needing a heart transplant is told by his doctor that the only heart available is that of a sheep.

The man finally agrees and the doctor transplants the sheep heart into the man.

A few days after the operation, the man comes in for a checkup.

The doctor asks him, "How are you feeling?"

The man replies, "Not BAAAAD."

The doctor says, "Madam, your husband needs rest and peace so here are some fast acting sleeping pills."

The wife asks, "When should I give them to him?"

The doctor replies, "The pills are for you."

A hospital posted a notice in the doctors' lounge that read, 'Remember, the first five minutes of a human being's life are the most dangerous.'

Underneath, a doctor had written, 'The last five are pretty risky, too.'

I went to the doctors last week, and he said, "Go to the coast for the weekend, it's great for 'flu."

So I went, and I got it.

A man rushed into a hospital and asked a doctor what was the best cure for hiccups.

Grabbing a cup of water, the doctor quickly splashed it into the man's face.

"What on earth did you that for?" screamed the man.

The doctor said, "You don't have the hiccups now, do you?"

"No I don't," replied the man. "My wife out in the car has them."

I was in hospital visiting my wife when the doctor suggested it might help if I adjusted my wife's pillows to make it more comfortable.

He was right.

Taking her pillows and putting them on my chair was a lot more comfortable for me.

A doctor came over to me he saw I was crying in the waiting room.

"What's wrong?" he asked.

"I don't believe it," I wept, "I reversed my car into my mother-in-law."

The doctor replied, "Sir, I can assure you that she'll be perfectly fine."

I said, "Exactly."

I went to the doctors the other day.

He said, "I'd like you to lie on the couch."

I said, "Why?"

He said, "I need to sweep the floor."

A nurse comes into the doctor's waiting room and says to the group of people waiting, "Due to new GDPR privacy rules I am not allowed to call you by your names. So, can the patient with syphilis, please come in."

It was time for my annual checkup.

Following the doctor's instructions, I collected a stool sample and put it in a plastic container before we left for the health center.

When I arrived, I handed the sample to the receptionist, who immediately cracked a smile.

The container read, 'I Can't Believe It's Not Butter.'

After my proctology exam I was left alone in the exam room for a few minutes.

A doctor then came in and said three words no man ever wants to hear.

He said, "Who was that?"

A very upset man spoke to his doctor.

"You've got to help me." he exclaimed.

The doctor questioned, "Just what seems to be the trouble?"

The man replied, "I keep having the same dream, every night. There's this door with a sign on it, and I push and push the door but I can't get it open."

The doctor asked, "What does the sign say?"

The man replied, "Pull."

A doctor took an elderly patient back to her room after surgery.

The woman was still feeling the effects of the anesthetic and was rather confused.

After the doctor had sure she was comfortable, he met one of the patient's friends who asked, "How is she?"

The doctor replied, "Oh, she's quite dozy."

The friend said, "I know that, but how is she health wise?"

A dog walks into a pub, and takes a seat at the bar. He says to the barman, "I would like a gin and tonic with lots of ice please."

The barman who has never heard a talking dog before says, "That's incredible; you should think about joining the circus."

The dog replies, "Why? Are they looking for doctors?"

A doctor tells his patient, "I have some good news and some bad news."

The patient says, "Give me the good news."

The doctor says, "You're about to have a disease named after you."

A doctor notices one of his hospital patients is in a panic so he asks what's wrong.

The patient says, "I'm due to have an operation but I over-heard the nurse say, 'It's a very simple operation, don't worry, I'm sure it will be all right.'"

The doctor asks, "What's so frightening about that?"

The guy replies, "She was talking to the surgeon."

I took my son to the hospital after he had swallowed some coins.

He was rushed into surgery.

Two hours later I saw a doctor so I asked him how my son was.

He said, "There's no change yet."

While visiting a friend in the hospital, I noticed several nurses were all wearing a pin designed to look like an apple.

I asked one of them, "What does the pin signify?"

"Oh, nothing," she replied with a chuckle. "We just use them to keep the doctors away."

A doctor enters the room of a difficult patient who demands to know the results of her examination.

He tells her, "I'm afraid I have some bad news. You're dying and you don't have much time left to live."

The woman says, "Oh no, that's dreadful news. How long have I got?"

"10..." says the doctor.

"10? 10 what? Months? Weeks? What?" she asks desperately.

The doctor replies, "10...9...8...7..."

A woman went for a routine physical examination at the hospital.

The nurse handed her a urine specimen container and said, "The bathroom is on your left. The doctor will be with you in a few minutes."

A few minutes later the lady came out of the bathroom with a relieved look on her face and an empty container.

She said to the nurse, "Thank you, but there was a toilet in there, so I didn't need this container after all."

A man speaks hysterically into the phone, "My wife is pregnant, and her contractions are only a couple of minutes apart."

"Is this her first child?" the nurse queries.

"No, you fool," the man screams. "This is her husband!"

One day a waiter fell sick and was rushed to hospital.

He was lying on the table in great pain.

When a doctor passed by the waiter said, "Hey doctor, could you do something for my pain?"

The doctor replied, "I'm sorry; this isn't my table."

I went to the doctors the other day.

He said, "You have got a very serious illness."

I said, "I want a second opinion."

He said, "OK, you're ugly as well."

A man is in hospital bed wearing an oxygen mask over his mouth.

The doctor on duty nurse hears him mumble, "Are my testicles black?"

The doctor lifts the patients gown, holds his manhood in one hand and his testicles gently in the other while he takes a closer look.

He then says, "There's nothing wrong with them, Sir."

The guy pulls off his oxygen mask, grimaces and says, "What I said was 'Are my test re-sults back?'"

A doctor took his cross-eyed dog to the vet.

The vet picked the dog up to examine him.

He checked his jaw, his joints and his eyes and then said, "I am going to have to put him down."

The doctor said, "Put him down? Just because he is cross eyed?"

The vet replied, "No, because he's very heavy."

After my prostate exam, the man in the white coat left me alone.

A few minutes late, the nurse came in, with a worried look on her face, and said the three words I was dreading to hear.

She said, "Who was that?"

An Asian nurse goes in to see a patient who has rung his bell.

A few minutes later she storms out, stating she refuses to deal with such a racist patient.

The doctor asks the patient what he said to upset the nurse.

He says, "I have no idea. She asked me if anything was bothering me, and I just said yeah, urination."

A mother complained to her doctor about her daughter's strange eating habits.

She said, "She lies in bed all day long and eats yeast and car wax. What will happen to her?"

"Ultimately," said the doctor, "she will rise and shine."

A doctor went in to check on a respiratory distress patient in the Critical Care Unit who was receiving oxygen via a mask.

The doctor talked to him, but the patient was gasping and unintelligible.

The doctor gave the patient a notepad and pencil and said, "I can't understand you. Please write down what the problem is."

The patient weakly scrawled on the pad, "Get your foot off my oxygen tube."

A young boy was brought into the emergency room after swallowing part of a plug-in air freshener.

After consulting the poisons unit and monitoring him, the doctor wrote on the boy's discharge note, 'Patient doing well. Ready to go home. Smells good.'

A doctor informed a patient's husband that his wife is comfortable.

The husband says, "I'm surprised. I thought she was in a coma and in a critical condition."

The doctor replies, "She is, the nurses are using her as a beanbag."

A patient was wheeled into the emergency room.

The doctor asked him, "On a scale of one to ten, with one representing minimal pain and ten representing excruciating pain, what would you say your pain level is?"

He thought for a second and then said, "I don't know. I'm not very good with math."

A new arrival, about to enter hospital, saw two doctors in white coats searching amongst the flower beds.

"Excuse me," he said, "have you lost something?"

"No," replied one of the doctors. "We're doing a heart transplant for an income-tax inspector and we are trying to find a suitable stone."

A man came to hospital with 70% burns.

The doctor says to the nurse attending him, "Give him a Viagra tablet."

The nurse asks, "Do you really think that Viagra will help?"

The doctor replies, "No, but it will keep the sheets off his legs."

A middle aged woman is walking her dog she notices a contented little man rocking in a chair on his porch.

She says, "I can't help noticing how happy you look. What is your secret for a long happy life?"

He replies, "I smoke three packs of cigarettes a day, I drink a bottle of scotch very day, I eat fatty foods, and I never exercise."

The woman says, "That's amazing. Just how old are you?"

The guy on the porch replies, "Twenty seven."

A doctor complained to his friend that his wife doesn't satisfy him anymore.

His friend advised he find another woman on the side.

When they met up a month or so later, the doctor told his friend, "I took your advice. I found a woman on the side, yet my wife still doesn't satisfy me."

I went to the doctors the other day.

I said, "I can't pronounce my F's, T's and H's."

The doctor replied, "Well you can't say fairer than that."

A doctor and a nurse were called to the scene of an accident.

The doctor says, "We need to get these people to hospital."

The nurse asks, "What is it?"

The doctor replies, "It's a big building with a lot of medical staff in it."

Paddy's wife was ready to give birth so he rushes her to the hospital.

When they arrive the doctor asks him, "How dilated is she?"

Paddy replies, "Oh Jaysus, she's over the moon."

I went to the doctors the other day.

He said, "What appears to be the problem?"

I replied, "I keep having a recurring dream, every night where many beautiful girls are rushing towards me and I keep pushing them away."

He asked, "How can I help?"

I replied, "Break my arms."

A doctor notices a stand in the mall that says, 'Brains for sale.'

He goes over to investigate and sees a sign that read, 'Paramedic brains $15 a pound, doctors brains $30 a pound and lawyers brains $150 a pound.'

She asks the brain seller, "How come a doctor's brains are worth 30 dollars and yet a lawyer's are worth 150?"

The man replies, "Have you any idea just how many lawyers it takes to make a pound of brains?"

A strung out woman goes to see her doctor.

The doctor asks her, "What is the problem?"

She rattles off, "When I woke up this morning, I looked at myself in the mirror and saw my skin was all wrinkled and pasty, my hair was all wiry and frazzled up, my eyes were completely bloodshot and bugging out, and I had this corpse-like look on my face. Just what is wrong with me?"

The doctor looks her over for a couple of minutes and then calmly says, "Well, I can tell you that there isn't anything wrong with your eyesight."

A doctor was showing some student doctors through the hospital.

At one point he stops and says to the junior doctors, "This will be the most hazardous section in the hospital for you. The men on this floor are almost well."

The hospital nurse brought a breakfast tray to a guy who was a bit of a practical joker.

The nurse also gave him a urine bottle to fill saying she'd pick it up when she came back to pick up the tray.

The patient, seeing some apple juice on the tray, decided for a bit of fun he would pour the juice into the specimen glass.

Later, when the nurse came back to pick up the specimen, she held it up to the light and said, "This looks a little cloudy. Are you feeling okay?"

The patient reached out his hand for the glass and said, "I'll run it through again, maybe I can filter it better this time." and he then drank it.

The nurse fainted.

A man went to the doctor as he was suffering with a wretched cold.

The doctor prescribed some medicine, but it didn't work.

On his subsequent visit the doctor gave the patient an injection, but that didn't help cure the cold either.

On his third visit the doctor said, "Go home and take a long hot bath. After you have finished bathing go into the bedroom, open the windows and stand in the draft."

The patient protested, "If I do that, I will probably get pneumonia."

The doctor said, "That's right, but I know I can cure pneumonia."

A man goes to the doctors.

The doctor says, "Go over to the window and stick your tongue out."

The man asks, "Why?"

The doctor replies, "I don't like my neighbors."

One day, an elderly man went to see his doctor and told him that he hadn't been feeling at all well.

The doctor examined him, left the room, and came back with three different bottles of pills.

Looking at the patient he says, "Take the green pill with a big glass of water when you wake up. Take the blue pill with a big glass of water after lunch. Take the red pill with another large glass of water after dinner."

Startled to be told to take so much medicine, the man stammered, "What exactly is my problem?"

The doctor replied, "You're not drinking enough water."

A doctor tells his patient who is struggling with his breathing, "Breathe in deeply and slowly exhale, and do it three times in total."

The patient does as he is requested.

The doctor then asks, "What do you feel now?"

The patient replies, "Your aftershave is simply overpowering."

A male doctor was talking to two of his friends about their teenage daughters.

The first friend says, "I was cleaning up my daughter's room the other day and I found a pack of cigarettes. I didn't even know she smoked."

The second friend says, "That's nothing. I was cleaning up my daughter's room the other day and I found a half full bottle of Vodka. I didn't even know she drank."

The doctor says, "That's nothing. I was cleaning up my daughter's room the other day and I found a pack of condoms. I didn't even know she had a penis."

During a patient's two-week follow-up appointment with his cardiologist, he told his doctor that he was having trouble with one of his medications.

The doctor asked, "Which one?"

"The patch," he replied. "The nurse told me to put on a new one every six hours and now I'm running out of places to put it."

The doctor asked the man to undress and he discovered what he really hoped he wouldn't see.

Yes, the man had over fifty patches on his body.

Chapter 4: Doctor Patient Exchanges

Patient: What did the x-ray of my head show?
Doctor: Absolutely nothing.

Patient: I keep seeing spots before my eyes.
Doctor: Have you seen a doctor before?
Patient: No, just spots.

Patient: I feel like a hundred dollar bill.
Doctor: Go shopping. Change would do you good.

Doctor: Are you sexually active?
Patient: No, I just lie there.

Patient: I think I'm suffering from déjà vu.
Doctor: Didn't I see you the other day?

Patient: I feel like I'm turning into a bear.
Doctor: How long have you felt this way?
Patient: Ever since I was a cub.

Patient: I feel like a pack of cards.
Doctor: I'll deal with you later.

Patient: I've got wind. Can you give me something?
Doctor: Yes – here's a kite.

Patient: I have a problem with these pills you gave me for BO.
Doctor: What's wrong with them?
Patient: They keep slipping out from under my arms.

Patient: I keep thinking there are two of me.
Doctor: One at a time please.

Patient: I keep getting pains in the eye when I drink coffee.
Doctor: Try taking the spoon out.

Patient: I always see spots before my eyes.
Doctor: Did the new glasses help?
Patient: Yes, I now see the spots much clearer.

Patient: My son has swallowed a pen, what should I do?
Doctor: Use a pencil until I get there.

Patient: I've had a stomach ache since I ate that cheese.
Doctor: Did it smell funny when you unwrapped it?
Patient: I was supposed to unwrap it?

Patient: I keep seeing an insect spinning around.
Doctor: Don't worry; it's just a bug that's going around.

Patient: I feel like an apple.
Doctor: We must get to the core of this.

Patient: I think I'm a moth.
Doctor: Why did you come here?
Patient: I saw a light at the window.

Patient: I feel run down.
Doctor: What makes you say that?
Patient: The tire marks across my legs.

Patient: My sister here keeps thinking she's invisible.
Doctor: What sister?

Patient: I keep losing my temper with people.
Doctor: Tell me about your problem.
Patient: I just did, you stupid fool.

Patient: I feel like a racehorse.
Doctor: Take one of these every four laps.

Patient: When I donate blood I do not extract it. A nurse does it for me.
Doctor: Yes, but this is a sperm bank and it doesn't work that way here.

Patient: Will this ointment clear up my inflammation?
Doctor: I never make rash promises.

Doctor: I have some good news and some bad news. The bad news is, you have short-term memory loss.
Patient: Oh no. What's the bad news?

Patient: Can I have a second opinion?
Doctor: Of course, come back tomorrow.

Patient: What can you give me for flat feet?
Doctor: How about a bicycle pump?

Patient: I keep thinking I'm invisible.
Doctor: Who said that?

Patient: I feel like a dog.
Doctor: Sit!

Patient: Will I be able to play the piano after this operation?
Doctor: Yes, of course.
Patient: That's great because I couldn't play it before.

Doctor: Your cough sounds better today.
Patient: It should, I practiced all night.

Patient: My hair keeps falling out. Have you got anything to keep it in?

Doctor: How about a cardboard box?

Patient: I swallowed a bone.

Doctor: Are you choking?

Patient: No, I really did.

Patient: You have to help me out.

Doctor: Certainly, which way did you come in?

Patient: I tend to flush a lot.

Doctor: Don't worry; it's just a chain reaction.

Patient: I'm boiling up.

Doctor: Just simmer down.

Patient: I keep painting myself gold.

Doctor: Don't worry it's just a gilt complex.

Patient: I've broken my arm in two places.

Doctor: Well, don't go back to those places.

Patient: I think I'm a dog.

Doctor: How long have you felt like this?

Patient: Ever since I was a puppy.

Patient: I dream there are monsters under my bed, what can I do?

Doctor: Saw the legs off your bed.

Patient: I think I'm a yo-yo.

Doctor: Are you stringing me along?

Patient: I keep dreaming of bugs, creepy-crawlies, demons, ghosts, vampires and werewolves and yetis.

Doctor: Do you always dream in alphabetical order?

Patient: My little boy has just swallowed a roll of film.

Doctor: Let's hope nothing develops.

Patient: I'm becoming invisible.

Doctor: Yes, I can see you're not all there.

Patient: I keep thinking I'm a frog.

Doctor: What's wrong with that?

Patient: I think I'm going to croak.

Doctor: You seem to be in excellent health. Your pulse is as regular as clockwork.

Patient: That's because you've got your hand on my watch.

Patient: Everyone keeps ignoring me.

Doctor: Next please.

Patient: Some days I feel like a tee-pee and other days I feel like a wig-wam.

Doctor: You're too tents.

Patient: I feel like a pair of curtains.

Doctor: Pull yourself together.

Patient: I'm a burglar.

Doctor: Have you taken anything for it?

Patient: I'm on a diet and it's making me irritable. Yesterday I bit someone's ear off.

Doctor: Oh dear, that's a lot of calories.

Doctor: Good news. You have passed your hearing test.

Patient: Huh?

Patient: I keep thinking I'm a dog.

Doctor: Sit on the couch and we will talk about it.

Patient: But I'm not allowed up on the couch.

Patient: I've a split personality.

Doctor: Well, you'd better both sit down then.

Patient: I have had my appendix, my gallbladder, my tonsils, my varicose veins and my wisdom teeth taken out, but I still feel unwell.

Doctor: That's quite enough out of you.

Doctor: Would you like an appointment for next week?
Patient: No, I'm sick now.

Patient: I think I'm a bridge.
Doctor: What's come over you?
Patient: Five cars, a large truck and a bus.

Patient: I've got bad breath and smelly feet.
Doctor: It sounds like you have Foot and Mouth disease.

Patient: I keep thinking I'm a caterpillar.
Doctor: Don't worry you'll soon change.

Patient: I keep thinking I'm a snake about to shed its skin.
Doctor: Go behind the screen and slip into something more comfortable.

Patient: I've lost my memory.
Doctor: When did this happen?
Patient: When did what happen?

Patient: How can I cure my sleep walking?

Doctor: Sprinkle tin-tacks on your bedroom floor.

Patient: Will it hurt me?

Doctor: Only when you get the bill.

Patient: My daughter believes in preventative medicine.

Doctor: Oh, really?

Patient: Yes, she tries to prevent me from making her take it.

Patient: I'm having trouble with my breathing.

Doctor: I'll give you something that will soon put a stop to that.

Patient: I keep thinking I'm a woodworm.

Doctor: How boring for you.

Patient: Everyone thinks I'm a liar.

Doctor: I can't believe that.

Patient: I can't stop my hands shaking.

Doctor: Do you drink a lot?

Patient: Not really. I spill most of it.

Patient: I think I've swallowed a pillow.

Doctor: How do you feel?

Patient: A little down in the mouth.

Patient: I can't get to sleep.

Doctor: Sit on the edge of the bed and you'll soon drop off.

Patient: I keep seeing double.

Doctor: Please sit on the couch.

Patient: Which one?

Patient: If I give up wine, women, and song, will I live longer?

Doctor: Not really. It will just seem longer.

Patient: How can I live to be a hundred?

Doctor: I suggest you give up eating rich food and going out with women.

Patient: And then will I live to be a hundred?

Doctor: No - but it will seem like it.

Doctor: You've got hypochondria.

Patient: Oh no, not that as well.

Patient: Have you got anything for my liver?

Doctor: What about some onions?

Patient: I get heartburn every time I eat birthday cake.

Doctor: Next time, take off the candles.

Patient: If I take these little yellow pills exactly as you suggested, will I get better?

Doctor: Let's put it this way - none of my patients has ever come back for more of those pills.

Patient: I've got a terrible pain in my right arm.

Doctor: Don't worry, it's just old age.

Patient: In that case, why doesn't my left arm hurt, too - I've had it just as long?

Patient: I keep hearing a ringing sound.

Doctor: Then answer the phone.

Patient: I think I'm an electric eel.

Doctor: That's shocking.

Patient: Will I be able to swim after this operation?

Doctor: Yes

Patient: Great, I couldn't before.

Patient: I feel like a cloud is following me.

Doctor: You do look like you are under the weather.

Receptionist: There's a patient here who says he's invisible.

Doctor: Tell him I can't see him right now.

Patient: When I pass from one country to another I have to get drunk.

Doctor: You're a borderline alcoholic.

Doctor: I'm afraid your DNA is backwards.

Patient: And?

ER Doctor: So, what brings you here?

Patient: An ambulance.

Patient: I've swallowed a tea spoon.

Doctor: Sit down and don't stir.

Patient: I think I'm pregnant.

Doctor: But I gave you the Pill.

Patient: Yes, I know. But it keeps falling out.

Patient: I think I've got tennis elbow.

Female Doctor: How many days have you had that?

Patient: Fifteen, love.

Patient: I keep thinking I'm a greenhouse.

Doctor: What symptoms do you have?

Patient: I've got panes all over.

Doctor: I've got the results of your test; you have onomatopoeia.

Patient: What's onomatopoeia?

Doctor: It's exactly what it sounds like.

Doctor: Did you know that there are more than a thousand bones in the human body?

Receptionist: Keep your voice down. There are two dogs outside.

Receptionist: There is a man in the waiting room with a glass eye named Brown.

Doctor: What does he call his other eye?

Nurse: There's some writing on this patient's foot.

Doctor: Yes, that's a footnote.

Nurse: The doctor is so funny he'll soon have you in stitches.

Patient: I hope not - I only came in for a checkup.

Patient: I think I need glasses.

Barber: I think so too - this is a hairdressing salon.

Chapter 5: Longer Doctor Jokes

On The Golf Course

A man staggered into a hospital with multiple bruises, a black eye and a golf club wrapped tightly around his throat.

Naturally, the doctor asked him what had happened.

The injured guy replied, "I was playing a round of golf with my wife, when at the fourth hole, she sliced her ball into a farmers field. We went to look for her ball and while I was looking around I noticed that one of the cows had something white at its rear end."

He continued, "I walked over to the cow, lifted up its tail, and would you believe it, there was my wife's monogrammed golf ball in the middle of the cow's butt."

"I held the cow's tail up and I shouted to my wife, 'Hey honey, this looks like yours.'"

"I don't remember too much after that."

Pulling Power

Carlo the property developer and his doctor buddy Doug, went bar-hopping every weekend together, and every week Carlo would go home with a woman while Doug went home alone.

One week Doug asked Carlo his secret to picking up women.

"That's easy," said Carlo, "When you're chatting to her and she asks you what you do for a living, don't tell her you're a doctor. Tell her you're a lawyer."

Later Doug is dancing with a woman when she leans in and asks him what he does for a living.

"I'm a lawyer," says Doug.

The woman smiles seductively and asks, "Want to go back to my place? It's just around the corner."

They go to her place, have some fun and an hour or so later, Doug is back in the pub telling Carlo about his success.

"I've only been a lawyer for an hour," Doug snickered, "And I've already screwed someone!"

Skipping

A blonde is overweight, so her doctor puts her on a diet.

He says, "I want you to eat regularly for two days, then skip a day, and repeat the procedure for two weeks. The next time I see you, you'll have lost at least ten pounds."

When the blonde returns, she tells the doctor that she has lost twenty two pounds.

"That' great news," the doctor says. "Did you follow my instructions?"

The blonde replies, "Yes I did. I thought I was going to drop dead on that third day though."

"From hunger, you mean?" asked the doctor.

"No, from all that skipping," replied the blonde.

The Duck Hunt

Five doctors went on a duck hunt: a GP, a pediatrician, a psychiatrist, a surgeon, and a pathologist.

After a while a bird came flying overhead, the GP raised his shogun but didn't shoot because he wasn't sure if it was a duck or not.

The pediatrician also raised his gun, but then he wasn't sure if it was a male or female duck, so he didn't shoot either.

The psychiatrist raised his gun and then thought, "I know that's a duck, but does the duck know that it is a duck?"

The surgeon was the only one who shot.

Boom! He blew the bird out of the sky.

He then turned to the pathologist and said, "Go and see if that was a duck."

A Postcard From Italy

A doctor was having an affair with one of the nurses at the hospital.

Shortly afterwards, she told him that she was pregnant.

Not wanting his wife to know, he gave the nurse some money and asked her to go to Italy and have the baby there.

She agreed and asked, "How will I let you know when the baby is born?"

He replied, "Send me a postcard and write 'spaghetti' on the back."

One day, some six months later, the doctor's wife called him at the office and said, "Darling, you have received a strange postcard in the mail from Europe today, and I don't understand what it means."

The doctor said, "I will read it when I get home later."

When the doctor came home that evening he read the postcard, and immediately had a heart attack.

He was rushed him to the hospital, where a medic comforted the wife and asked her what trauma had precipitated the cardiac arrest.

The wife explained that he had simply read a postcard from Italy.

The medic was confused so he read the postcard out loud, "Spaghetti, Spaghetti, Spaghetti - Two with sausage and meatballs, one without."

Reunion

A group of doctors, all aged 40, discussed where they should meet for lunch. They agreed that they would all convene at Giovanni's restaurant as the waitresses who worked there were friendly and they wore short-skirts.

Ten years later, at age 50, the doctors once again discussed where they should meet for lunch.

It was agreed that they would meet at Giovanni's because the food and service was good and there was an excellent wine list.

Ten years later, at age 60, the friends again discussed where they should meet for lunch.

It was agreed that they would meet at Giovanni's because there were plenty of parking spaces, they could dine in peace and quiet, and it was good value for money.

Ten years later, at age 70, the doctors, now all retired, discussed where they should meet for lunch.

It was agreed that they would meet at Giovanni's because the restaurant was wheelchair accessible and had a toilet for the disabled.

Ten years later, at age 80, the friends discussed where they should meet for lunch.

Finally it was agreed that they would meet at Giovanni's because they had never been there before.

The Hairy Cop

A policeman was rushed to the hospital with an inflamed appendix.

The doctors operated and afterwards advised him that all was well.

However, the cop felt something pulling at the hairs on his chest.

He decided to pull his hospital gown down enough so that he could see what was making him uncomfortable.

Taped firmly across his hairy chest were four wide strips of adhesive tape, the kind that doesn't come off easily.

Written in large black letters was the sentence, 'Get well soon. From the doc you gave a speeding ticket to last week.'

Dyslexic Nurse

A doctor is doing the rounds on the ward with a dyslexic nurse.

They come to a bed where the patient is laying half dead.

"Did you give this man two tablets every eight hours?" asks the doctor.

"Oops," replies the nurse, "I gave him eight tablets every two hours."

At the next bed the next patient also appears half dead.

The doctor asks, "Nurse, did you give this man one tablet every twelve hours?"

"Oops, I gave him twelve tablets every one hour," replies the nurse.

Unfortunately at the next bed the patient is well and truly deceased, not an ounce of life.

"Nurse," asks the doctor, "did you prick his boil?"

"Oops." replies the nurse.

The Pain of Childbirth

A woman goes into labor with her first child.

The doctor tells her and her husband that they have invented a new device to transfer the pain of child birth to the father.

The doctor asks the husband for his approval to use the new device.

He agrees and so the doctor turns the pain up to 10%.

The man feels nothing.

The doctor increases the pain level to 20%.

The guy still feels nothing.

The doctor keeps increasing the pain level in the device right up to 100%.

The man still feels nothing.

He left his wife in the hospital with their new born baby, and he went home happy.

When he got home, he found the milkman dead on the porch.

Near Death Experience

A middle-aged woman had a heart attack and was rushed to hospital.

While on the operating table she had a near death experience.

Seeing God, she asked, "Is my time up?"

God replied, "No, you have another 20 years, 3 months and 4 days to live."

After recovering from her surgery, the woman decided to stay in the hospital and have a facelift, liposuction, and a tummy tuck.

She even went to the hair salon and changed her hair color, figuring that as she had plenty of time to live, she might as well make the most of it.

On the day of her release from hospital, she crossed the street and was hit by a car and unfortunately died instantly.

Arriving in Heaven in front of God, she exclaimed, "I thought you said that I had another 20 years to live. Why did you let that car run me over?"

God replied, "I didn't recognize you."

Patel's Accident

There was once a Gujarati living in California named Raju Patel, who was involved in a car accident. At the hospital, when he awoke, he called for the doctor to tell him what had happened to him.

The nurse said, "I'm very sorry, sir, but you were involved in a serious car accident."

"Accident! Is my Mercedes all right?" he asked hysterically.

The nurse said, "I am sorry but your car was destroyed. However that is the least of your worries - you lost your left arm in the crash, and we were unable to save it."

He screams, "I lost my arm? My Rolex! My Rolex!"

The nurse says, "Please calm down. That is the least of your worries. You remain in a critical condition, but all your family are here to see you, and they are waiting outside."

He asked for his family to be called in.

As they gathered around the bed, he called for each of them by name.

"Shilpa, are you here?"

"I am here husband, and I will never leave you."

"Anil, my child, are you here?"

"I am here father, and I will never leave you."

"Dilip, my child, are you here?"

"I am here father, and I will never leave you."

"Priya, my child, are you here?"

"I am here father, and I will never leave you."

"Well," said Raju thoughtfully, "if Shilpa, Anil, Dilip and Priya are here, who the heck is in the shop?"

Following Orders

A doctor briefed a nurse on a patient's condition.

The doctor said, "This patient is a good golfer. His injury is serious and I fear he will not be able to play golf again unless you follow my orders exactly."

The doctor then began listing orders, "You must give an injection in his left leg every 90 minutes, followed by a second injection exactly five minutes after the first. He must take two pills exactly every hours, followed by one pill every 15 minutes for eight hours. He must drink no more and no less than 10 ounces of water every 30 minutes. Every two hours, soak his arm in warm water for 15 minutes, and then place on ice for 10 minutes. He requires a back rub every hour. Feed him a low sugar low carb meal three times a day. Chart his condition and vital signs every 20 minutes. You must do these things exactly or his injury will not heal properly, and he will not able to play golf again."

The doctor left and the nurse entered the patient's room to be greeted by anxious family members and an equally anxious patient.

The patient asked what the doctor had said and the nurse replied, "The doctor said that you will live."

She then quickly added, "But you will have to learn a new sport."

Three New Fathers

Three expectant fathers were in a Minneapolis hospital waiting room while their wives were in labor.

The nurse arrived and proudly announced to the first guy, "Congratulations. You're the new father of twins."

The guy said, "What a coincidence. I work for the Doublemint Chewing Gum Company."

Later the nurse returned and congratulated the second father on the birth of his triplets.

The guy said, "Well, how about that? I work for the 3M Corporation."

After this, the others turned to look at the third guy who promptly fainted.

The nurse rushed to his side to bring him round and comfort him.

As he slowly gained consciousness, the others heard him whisper, "I need some fresh air. I work for 7-Up."

Chapter 6: Rude and Risqué Doctor Jokes

If you are easily offended, it's best to skip this chapter.

A doctor and his nurse wife had a big argument over breakfast about their sex life.

"You know, you are not very good in bed." the husband shouted before he stormed off to work.

By the afternoon, he decided he'd better apologize so he phoned home to talk to his wife.

After many rings, she picked up the phone.

He asked, "Why did you so take so long to answer the phone?"

She replied, "I was in bed."

He asked, "What are you doing in bed at this time of day?"

She replied, "Getting a second opinion."

A doctor friend of mine decided to have a prostate test carried out while he was visiting Thailand.

He was asked to strip off and to lay naked on his side on the couch.

After he had done so, the nurse began the examination.

After a minute, the nurse said, "At this stage of the procedure it's quite normal to get an erection."

My friend said, "I haven't got an erection."

"Well I have," replied the nurse.

I applied to be a sperm donor and the doctor asked if I could masturbate in the cup.

I told him that I'm pretty good but I don't think I am ready to compete in a tournament yet.

A woman patient in a hospital had been in a coma for a few weeks.

One day while washing her private parts a nurse notices that the monitor showed an increase in her heart rate.

The nurse tells the doctor who studies the results before telephoning the patient's husband asking him to come in.

When he arrives the doctor suggests that oral sex may help.

The husband agrees and the doctor pulls the curtain around the bed for privacy.

Thirty minutes later the monitor shows that her heart and breathing has stopped, and she flat lines and unfortunately dies.

The doctor rushes in to ask the husband what happened.

He just simply says, "I don't know, maybe she choked."

"Of course I won't laugh," said the doctor. "I'm a professional. In over twenty years I have never laughed at a patient."

"OK then," said the patient.

He then proceeded to undo his trousers and underwear, revealing the smallest penis the doctor had ever seen in her life.

The doctor was simply unable to control herself, and she giggled.

Feeling awful that he had laughed at the man's genitals, he composed herself as well as he could.

"I'm very sorry," he said, "I don't know what came over me. I promise it won't happen again. Now tell me, what is the problem?"

The patient replied, "It's swollen."

The doctor had to leave the room.

A female doctor was making her rounds at the insane asylum.

Her first stop is a man with his dick in his hands and was swinging it like a baseball bat.

She asks, "What are you doing?"

He replies, "I'm Babe Ruth, the world's most famous baseball player."

She continues to the next room where she sees the patient holding his dick like a golf club.

She asks, "What are you doing?"

He replies, "I'm Tiger Woods, the world's most famous golfer."

On to the next room she peeks in and she sees a guy balancing a peanut on the tip of his dick.

She asks, "Who are you supposed to be?"

He replies, "Who me? I'm just f*cking nuts."

Chapter 7: Things You Don't Want to Hear During Surgery

- Has anyone seen my watch?
- Has anyone ever survived 500ml of this stuff before?
- There go the lights again.
- That was some party last night. I can't remember when I've been that drunk.
- OK, now take a picture from this angle. This is truly a freak of nature.
- If I can just remember how they did this on ER.
- I wish I hadn't forgotten my glasses.
- What do you mean he wasn't in for a sex change.
- Did this patient sign the organ donation card?
- Don't worry. I think it is sharp enough.
- Better save that. We'll need it for the autopsy.
- Wait a minute, if this is his spleen, then what's that?
- I don't know what it is, but pack it in ice.
- Hurry up, I want to miss all the traffic.
- This laughing gas is funny. Can I have some more?
- Of course I've performed this operation before.

Chapter 8: Doctors Pick-Up Lines

You raise my dopamine levels.

Want to go and study some anatomy?

You should get your own temperature. You look hot.

Are you my appendix? I have a gut feeling I should take you out.

Blood is red, cyanosis is blue, I get tachycardia when I think of you.

ICU in my dreams.

The way you talk to me leaves me aphasic.

I'm an expert at mouth-to-mouth.

I just want to swab you up and down, then left and right, until we're both afebrile.

Emphysema puffs pink, chronic bronchitis makes you blue, but no COPD makes me as breathless as you.

Are you a C-reactive protein? Because you have a-cute phase.

You're systemic and I'm pulmonary. Though we may be divided, together we are one.

You'd better be a cardiologist, because something about you makes me want to give you my heart.

You take my breath away.

I hope someday I will be your emergency contact.

Let's exchange genetic information.

Can you hear what my heart is saying?

I want to be an organ donor. I want to give my heart to you.

When we first met I couldn't get you out of my mind, now I can't get you out of my heart.

You can feel for my pulse whenever you like.

Chapter 9: Bumper Stickers for Doctors

Proud to be a doctor.

Doctors do it for twelve hours straight.

I'm a doctor, not a magician.

Please don't take your organs to heaven. Heaven knows we need them here.

Maybe you can't see it, but a doctor can.

Eat. Sleep. Save lives. Repeat.

Doctors call the shots.

Doctors are I.V. Leaguers.

Chapter 10: Summary

That's pretty well it for this book. I hope you've enjoyed this collection of doctors jokes. As you know, some were cheesy but I hope they brought a smile to your face, and you found them *humerus* and they tickled *your funny bone*.

I've written plenty of other joke books and here are just a few gags from a book of mine unpretentiously titled 'The Punniest Joke Book Ever' which is available exclusively on Amazon:-

Trying to write with a broken pencil is pointless.

My wife has thrown me out because of my obsession with Arnold Schwarzenegger quotes. I told her, "I'll be back."

Global warming. Is it just hot air?

When I die, I would like the word 'humble' inscribed on the base of my statue.

About the Author

Chester Croker, known to his friends as Chester the Jester or Croker the Joker, has written many joke books, and has twice been named Comedy Writer of the Year by the International Jokers Guild. During his schoolboy days he took voluntary service as a hospital porter and he is the significant other of a wonderful nurse, who has provided him with plenty of material for this book.

He can be followed on twitter @ChesterCroker if that's your thing.

If you did enjoy the book, please leave a review on Amazon so that other doctors can have a good laugh too.

Many thanks in advance.

Printed in Great Britain
by Amazon